THE MODE OF BAPTISM:

A DISCOURSE

DELIVERED IN THE

Congregational Church, of Jackson, Mich.,

APRIL 18, 1869, AND REPEATED APRIL 25, 1869.

By REV. J. W. HOUGH.

JACKSON, MICH.:
JAMES O'DONNELL, STEAM BOOK AND JOB PRINTER.
1869.

THE MODE OF BAPTISM:

From the Author to
W. E. C

A DISCOURSE

DELIVERED IN THE

First Congregational Church, of Jackson, Mich.,

APRIL 18, 1869, AND REPEATED APRIL 25, 1869.

By REV. J. W. HOUGH.

JACKSON, MICH.:
JAMES O'DONNELL, STEAM BOOK AND JOB PRINTER.
1869.

CORRESPONDENCE.

JACKSON, MICH., April 20, 1869.

Rev. J. W. Hough—Dear Sir: We, the undersigned, expressing the sentiments of many others, would request that you will repeat the sermon on Baptism, preached last Sabbath, on the next Sabbath evening, or at your earliest convenience; and we would also request a copy of the same for publication.

GEO. H. LATHROP, J. M. HOLLAND,
A. S. CUSHMAN, CHAS. H. BENNETT,
M. A. McNAUGHTON, L. KASSICK,
W. C. LEWIS, V. M. BOSTWICK,
E. H. RICE.
L. T. OSBORN, GEO. F. RICE,

JACKSON, April 22, 1869.

My Dear Friends—Your note is before me. The sermon to which you refer, was prepared in the ordinary course of my pulpit work, and for my own congregation only, yet, upon your judgment that its repetition and publication would be useful, I cheerfully comply with your wishes. I will repeat the discourse on Sabbath evening next, and then place the manuscript in your hands.

I am, Brethren,

Yours in Christian service,

J. W. HOUGH.

Messrs. Geo. H. Lathrop and others.

The like figure whereunto even baptism doth also now save us, (not the putting away of the filth of the flesh, but the answer of a good conscience toward God.)—I. *Pet.*, 3: 21.

Baptism is a "saving ordinance." The doctrine of "baptismal regeneration," so often condemned as heresy, is nevertheless taught in the Scriptures. In fact, the Scriptures plainly teach that there is no regeneration but baptismal regeneration. No unbaptized person can be saved. This strong uncompromising doctrine, that baptism is absolutely essential to salvation, was taught by Christ himself, and often reiterated by the Apostles. Not repentance, not faith, was more stoutly insisted upon as a necessary condition of eternal life, than was baptism.

It should ever be kept in mind,—and is almost always forgotten,—that there are two baptisms: inner and outer; having precisely that relation to each other, which the soul has to the body, and ranking in relative importance as the soul and the body rank. The one is the substance, the other is only the shadow of it. The real baptism, the substance, has to do with the soul; the shadow baptism, or symbol, has to do with the body. Baptism in its inner significance, as Christ held and taught it, is the cleansing of the soul from its sin by the blood of Jesus. This is the real baptism, the regeneration of the spiritual nature from its sin by the Holy Ghost. "I indeed baptize you with water," said John, "but He that cometh after me shall baptize you with the Holy Ghost." Baptism with the Holy Ghost is regeneration. It is the cleansing of the soul by the blood of Christ. This is the real baptism, and this, as I have already said, is a "saving ordinance." No man is ever saved who has not been baptized by the blood of Christ. Every man who has been baptized by the blood of Christ will be saved. "Baptism doth save," says our text, but goes on immediately to distinguish between the two baptisms, not the baptism of the body, "not the putting away of the filth of the flesh," but the cleansing of the inward man,—this is what saves, "the answer of a good conscience toward God." The Bible carefully distinguishes between these two baptisms, and men continually confound them together. "According to His mercy He saved us, by the washing of regeneration, and the renewal of the Holy Ghost." This is plainly the baptism of the soul. "See, here is water: what doth hinder me to be baptized?" This is as plainly the baptism of the body. "Having our hearts sprinkled from an evil conscience, (baptism of the soul,) and our bodies washed with pure water" (baptism of the body). "Except a man be born of water and of the Spirit, he cannot enter into the kingdom of God." (Both baptisms in one sentence.) "One Lord, one faith, one baptism." (Baptism of the soul, one Savior, one faith in Him, one baptism by His blood;—saving faith and saving baptism.) "He that believeth, and is baptized, shall be saved." (Baptism of the soul. If we read, "He that believeth, and is *regenerated*, shall be saved," we do not change the sense in the least.) "For by one spirit are we all baptized into one body." (Baptism of the soul by the Spirit, not baptism of the body by man.)

I repeat, there are two baptisms, inner and outer: the baptism of the soul by the blood of Christ, and the baptism of the body by water. Still farther, the baptism of the soul is the more important, just as much more important than the baptism of the body, as the soul itself is of more importance than the body. This distinction, indeed, is not limited to this matter of baptism; it is as broad as the whole scope of our religious life. It is simply the recognition of the fact that our life is two-fold, inner and outer. We have the same distinction applied *e. g.* to the other ordinance of the Lord's Supper—"Except ye eat the flesh of the Son of man, and drink His blood, ye have no life in you." (This is the inner communion of the soul with Christ, absolutely essential to salvation.) "As oft as ye eat this bread, and drink this cup, ye do shew the Lord's death till He come." (This is the outer, bodily symbol, not essential to salvation.) The two rank in importance as the soul and the body rank. The baptism of the soul is essential to salvation; the baptism of the body is not. Baptism by the blood of Christ saves; baptism by water does not. Whoso has been baptized by the blood of Christ has been really baptized. He may never have been baptized by water, but his heart has been "sprinkled from an evil conscience." He has been baptized by the Holy Ghost, though not by human hands.

And here I pause to say, that this distinction, drawn wholly from the Scriptures, breaks the force of the argument used by our Baptist brethren, in all good conscience without doubt, to establish what is commonly known as "close communion." When they urge that none should commune but those who have been baptized, we agree with them. When they go farther to urge that none may in any case commune but those who have been baptized with water, we dare not go with them. Christ sat down with the twelve at the sacramental table, although there is nothing in the gospels, not even a line, to show that any one of the twelve had ever been baptized with water. Indeed, Christian baptism, baptism "in the name of the Father, and of the Son, and of the Holy Ghost," had not even been instituted at the time when our Lord and the twelve ate the Supper. After the Supper, after the betrayal, after the crucifixion and burial, and resurrection, after the repeated appearances to His disciples, our Lord gave to them this last command: "Go ye, therefore, and teach all nations, baptizing them in the name of the Father, and of the Son, and of the Holy Ghost." Up to this time there had been no baptism "in the name of the Father, and of the Son, and of the Holy Ghost." Indeed, the Holy Ghost had not yet been given. Ohlsausen, commenting on our Savior's last command, (Matt., 28: 19, 20,) says, "In the 19th verse there follows the important *institution of the sacrament of baptism*. . . . It is plain that our Lord intended to institute a *perpetual* rite which should be binding upon the church in all ages, and in which alike baptism and teaching refer to *all nations*. From this it follows, therefore, that the baptism ordained by Christ differed essentially from the baptism of John, which possessed but a temporary significance. The Christian sacrament of baptism was not to be merely a baptism of repentance, but rather a symbol of the second birth." In a note he adds, that the earlier baptism administered by the disciples (John, 4: 2,) "was not essentially different from the baptism of John." Lange, discussing the same passage, says: "With this apostolic commission, and *with the institution of baptism, which had been preceded by that of the Supper*, and of the ministerial office, and by the presentation of the keys, the institution of the Church is finished."

Obviously the sacrament of the Lord's Supper was instituted before that of baptism. Our Lord sat down at the communion-table with the twelve although they had not received Christian baptism. Our Baptist brethren refuse to sit at the Lord's table with those whom they acknowledge to be genuine disciples of Christ, unless they have first been totally immersed in water. They are wont to insist much that we should imitate Christ's example literally in regard to the mode of baptism. Would it not be well for them, either to prove that the twelve had been immersed, or else to imitate Christ's example literally in admitting unimmersed persons to his table? If we were to grant that immersion were the only proper mode of water-baptism, it would by no means follow that none but the immersed may commune. Indeed, open-communion was held and taught by Robert Hall, the most eloquent man the Baptist ministry ever possessed; it is held by Spurgeon, the most eminent man in the denomination, to-day; it is largely practised by the Baptists of England, and (I venture the prediction,) it will yet be practiced by the Baptists of this country.

Christ took the thief on the cross at once into fullest fellowship, saying, "To-day shalt thou be with me in paradise." In the circumstances baptism with water was impossible, yet the penitent soul had been baptized by the blood of Christ, and Christ at once promised him a seat with himself at the marriage supper of the Lamb. Every regenerate soul is baptized by the blood of Christ, and every man baptized by Christ himself with His own blood is genuinely baptized, and will be received by Christ into full fellowship with himself. And no Church is better than Christ himself. No Church is at liberty persistently to reject from its fellowship and communion any whom it believes that Christ fellowships and communes with. If my Baptist brother says that, because I have not been immersed, I am therefore not a Christian, I have no word to say. I may differ from his opinion, but I have no longer any claim on him for fellowship. But if he says to me, "I have no doubt that you are a very good Christian brother; I love to hear you pray; I love to join with you in Christian labor; I expect ere long to sing God's praises with you in Heaven; I have no doubt that Christ fellowships and communes with you, but I cannot," then I reply, "I must be content to receive the fellowship of Christ, and to dispense with yours." I repeat, *no Church is at liberty persistently to reject from its fellowship and communion any whom it believes that Christ fellowships and communes with.*

The washing of regeneration, the sprinkling of the

heart from an evil conscience, the inner baptism of the soul by the blood of Christ, this is the essential baptism; this is the baptism that saves. In laying such stress upon this point I do not say, or imply, that the other baptism,—the outer baptism of water,—is of no importance. It is of very great importance, though not essential to salvation. It is highly important that a man should have two arms and two feet in this world, yet he may live if he have neither. The soul is essential, yet the body is the appointed instrument of all its earthly activity. Recognizing this distinction, Christ was wont to appoint for each spiritual fact its corresponding bodily symbol. The Holy Spirit had its physical symbol in the breath, (*spiritus*) and took its name therefrom. Spiritual communion with Christ had its outward symbol in the emblems of the Lord's Supper. The spiritual feeding upon Christ is essential to salvation; the eating and drinking of the bread and the wine are important and obligatory; yet many a man is redeemed who never sits at the Lord's table. So baptism is the inward spiritual fact of the cleansing of the soul from sin by the blood of Christ. And the application of water is enjoined as the fitting bodily symbol of this inward fact.

And here we come upon the vexed question of this whole subject:—In what mode should water be applied as the outward symbol of the inner baptism of the soul by the blood of Christ?

I. It was not like Christ to prescribe any mode in which water should be applied. His gospel was not in the least a gospel of modes or forms. Spiritual truths were everything to him, forms and ceremonies nothing. In the Jewish ritual everything was defined with the utmost nicety. The mode in which all things should be done was prescribed to the last point of particularity. The tabernacle was to be built after a certain pattern which was explained beforehand, down to the hanging of every curtain. The altar had its exact measurements. The whole furniture of the tabernacle was defined, to the candlesticks and the snuffers thereof. Every garment of the priest's dress was regulated by law. Every ordinance had the mode of its performance explicitly stated. The priest was instructed how to select the victim, and how to kill it, and what to do with the blood. The people were enjoined what they might eat, how they should mourn, how far they might walk on the Sabbath day.

The aim of these minutiæ was exclusiveness. The whole ceremonial service was to be an isolating power to keep the Jews distinct from the idolatrous nations about them. These peculiar customs and usages kept the Jews by themselves, and the other nations apart from them, as effectively as the initiatory rites and pass-words of a Free Mason's Lodge keep the uninitiated out and the initiated by themselves. Prescribed forms and exclusiveness always go hand in hand. The two bodies of Protestant Christians in our own day that lay stress upon forms, the one upon their form of liturgy, and the other upon their form of baptism, are the two that are exclusive toward other bodies of Christians. However kindly their feelings towards others, their adherence to forms inevitably makes them draw the line between themselves and those who do not conform to their usage.

Forms were prescribed to the Jews with the purpose to secure exclusiveness. The intent of Christianity, however, was wholly different. It was not to be exclusive but universal. Judaism was for one nation and one age; Christianity for all nations and all time. In it there was to be "neither Greek nor Jew, Barbarian, Scythian, bond nor free." Christ, therefore, in laying the foundations of it, steadily refused to enjoin upon his followers any forms, or modes of worship whatever. He dealt with principles, but never in prescriptions or regulations. Judaism said: "Worship in Jerusalem." "Nay," said Christ, "Worship is a thing of the heart, not of place." "The hour cometh when ye shall neither in this mountain, nor yet in Jerusalem worship the Father . . the true worshiper shall worship the father in spirit and in truth." He always laid stress upon the spirit of the worshipper, never on the place or the form of worship. He refused to lay down any definite polity, or form of church government, choosing instead to enunciate certain principles, capable of adaptation to all the varying circumstances of successive generations. He did not give directions how churches were to be built, nor prescribe any form of service according to which all were to worship. He did not use himself, nor bind upon his followers a form of prayer. He did not give any detailed directions as to the mode of administering the sacrament of the Lord's Supper. If he did prescribe any mode in which baptism was to be administered, it is the one solitary instance in which he prescribed any form, or mode of service, to his Church.

If we examine the teachings of the Apostles who were themselves taught by Christ, we find every where the same prominence given to spirituality, the same absence of all prescribed modes. In the Apostles' day questions of form perpetually occurred. Christians converted from Judaism were very naturally prone, because of their training, to lay stress upon forms. "Christians must be circumcised," said they. "They should observe the feasts." "They should not eat meat which has been offered to idols." "Nay," said the apostles; "In Jesus Christ neither circumcision availeth anything, nor uncircumcision; but faith which worketh by love." So of feast days. "He that regardeth the day, regardeth it unto the Lord; he that regardeth not the day, to the Lord he doth not regard it." They held this principle uniformly throughout. If any man's conscience bid him observe any form, then let him observe it; not for the form's sake, but for conscience' sake. The form is nothing, but the conscience everything. "Neither if we eat are we the better, neither if we eat not are we worse." "Let every man be fully persuaded in his own mind." "Where the spirit of the Lord is there is liberty." The gospel does not attempt to prescribe modes of administration. It presupposes "differences of administration," taking care only that there be in all "the same Lord." The grand requirement of Christianity is that every man should worship in spirit and in truth, but as to the mode of worship, he is at liberty to follow the dictates of his own conscience. If this be not the spirit of the whole New Testament, then I have utterly mistaken its teachings. I repeat, then, it would have been in direct contradiction to the spirit of all his teachings, and in opposition to the whole tenor of the gospel, if Christ had enjoined upon his followers any precise mode in which baptism was to be administered, and made that mode binding for all time.

II. I proceed further to say, that in point of fact he did not enjoin any specific mode in which water is to be applied in baptism. If he had wished to enjoin any such mode, he would have done it so clearly that "wayfaring men, though fools, should not err therein." He would have been at no loss for language so to express his wish that there would have been no room for mistake, or doubt, or controversy. The chapters of Leviticus and Deuteronomy are notable specimens of the divine ability to prescribe modes of administration. There was never any controversy as to how the tabernacle was to be built, for the Lord wished it built after a certain pattern, and he said so, explaining his wishes with a clearness and explicitness that left no possible space for misunderstanding. Had he felt it to be important that the mode of water-baptism should be defined, he would have defined it with equal explicitness, and made controversy equally impossible. Centuries of controversy, centuries of scholarly, profound, prayerful investigation, without bringing either the scholars themselves or the church at large, to any agreement as to what mode was prescribed, are proof absolute that no mode was prescribed. Controversy regarding doctrine may exist, since it is extremely difficult so to define doctrine, that men with differing minds will not conceive it differently. On the contrary, it is entirely easy to define a mode of administration perfectly. If the Lord had been desirous that all his followers should be totally submerged in water, five words would have made his wish so plain that all the Christian world must have been agreed upon it. Whereas, five-sixths of the Christian world are now honestly unable to see that such was our Lord's intention. If the Jews had honestly differed for hundreds of years as to whether the tabernacle should be built in this mode or that, what other conclusion could man have reached than this: Either the Lord made no attempt to explain how it was to be built, or else he signally failed in his explanation. The fact that conscientious men, learned and unlearned, honestly differ as to the mode of baptism, proves either that the Lord did not attempt to define the mode, or that his attempt was a wretched failure. Certain passages, taken alone and interpreted narrowly, seem to favor this mode, certain others favor that mode, bringing us again to the same result, that no attempt was made to define the mode. It is with this ordinance as with church polity. The Episcopalian singles out certain passages, and says, "There is Episcopacy for you, plainly enough." The Congregationalist singles out certain other passages, and says, "If the New Testament does n't teach Congregationalism, it does n't teach anything," the simple truth being that the New Testament makes no attempt to prescribe a church polity. It teaches certain principles, and then leaves church government, like civil government, to shape itself according to the diverse needs of the Church in different ages and circumstances. Precisely so, it appoints water-baptism, and leaves the Church to apply it by whatever mode seems fitting and best.

III. Christ did not prescribe immersion as the mode of applying water in baptism. I have already said that Christ did not prescribe any mode. I now single out immersion, because the claim is made that Christ did prescribe that as the only mode. It becomes necessary therefore to examine the arguments by which it is attempted to maintain this claim.

It is claimed that the Greek words *Bapto* and *Baptizo* always mean "to immerse." It is impossible here to enter upon an examination of the usage of these words by Greek authors outside of the Scriptures. Mr. Dale, in his recent work, entitled "Classic Baptism,"* has made a thorough investigation of this usage, grouping together all the principal passages in the whole range of Classic Greek in which these words are employed, and showing conclusively that they did not uniformly signify "to immerse."†

It concerns us more nearly, however, to inquire, Do these words invariably signify "to immerse" as they are employed in the New Testament? We shall find, I think, that they are there used to denote the application of water by different modes, as in the following passages:

Luke 11: 38, "The Pharisee . . . marvelled that he had not first washed before dinner." (In the original "*baptized* before dinner.") But the method of "*baptizing*" before dinner practised in the East, then and now, is not to dip the hands in the water, but to pour water on the hands.‡ Baptizing, then, may be performed by pouring.

---

* *Classic Baptism:* An Inquiry into the Meaning of the Word *Baptizo* as determined by the Usage of Classical Greek Writers. By JAMES W. DALE, Pastor of the Media Presbyterian Church, Del. Co., Pa. Boston: Draper & Halliday, 1867; pp. 354.

† Dr. Alexander Carson, one of the ablest defenders of the Immersionist view, while laboring to prove that these words always signify "to immerse," makes this frank confession, "all the lexicographers and commentators are against me in that opinion." Cox and Carson; page 79.

Another writer says, "I have consulted between twenty and thirty different lexicons upon this subject, not one of which gives dip, plunge, or immerse, as the exclusive meaning of these words." Conklin—*Seventeen Reasons for not becoming a Close-Communion Baptist.*

‡ See the mode of washing illustrated in *The Land and the Book*, I. p. 184;

Mark 7 : 4, "When they come from the market, except they wash, (Grk. *baptize*) they eat not. And many other things there be which they have received to hold, as the washing (Grk. *baptisms*) of cups and pots, brasen vessels and of tables." The reference here is obviously to a ceremonial cleansing of household utensils, practised by the Pharisees in obedience to "the tradition of the elders," an unwarranted and needless ceremonial cleansing, it is true, yet derived from and in imitation of that required by the Mosaic ritual. But the ceremonial cleansing required by the Mosaic ritual was performed by sprinkling, never by immersion. When, therefore, the Evangelist speaks of the Jews as accustomed to baptize cups and pots, brasen vessels and tables, we do not understand that they immersed them in water.

In I. Cor. 10 : 2, we read that the Israelites "were all baptized unto Moses in the cloud, and in the sea." The Baptist is here compelled by his theory to translate, they "were all *immersed* unto Moses in the cloud, and in the sea," whereas we know from the history that the cloud went before them, and that they went through the sea on dry ground. Nothing is more entirely clear than that they were not immersed either in the cloud or in the sea. The Baptist, if he would be consistent, is shut up by his theory to the absurdity of saying that they were immersed in the sea on dry land !*

Comp. Bib. Researches in Palestine, III. pp. 86, 230. See also 1. Kings, 3 : 11. When in Syria my own hands were "*baptized*" after this mode, in the house of Abu Selim, in Tripoli. One of his daughters brought a pitcher and napkin, and poured water on the hands, while another held the "*tusht*," or basin, beneath them.

* Dr. Gill, commenting upon this passage, supposes that the cloud, as it passed over the Israelites in the camp, "let down a plentiful rain upon them, whereby they were *in such a condition as if they had been all over dipped in water*," a supposition which, if it had any shadow of foundation, would warrant the inference that immersion may be performed by a thorough sprinkling. As to the baptism in the sea, he explains that as the wall of water stood up higher than their heads, "*they seemed to be immersed in it*," which *seems* much like admitting that the word does not always signify total submersion in water.

But we are told that Christ must have been immersed, since we read that he was "baptized of John in [*en*] Jordan," and that he went "straightway up out of [*apo*] the water." But the use of these prepositions is by no means decisive as to the fact of immersion. The preposition translated "in" is often translated "at," *e. g.* "*at* the right hand of God," (Rom., 8: 34.) So, the word rendered "out of" is translated "from" five times as often as "out of" throughout the first five books of the New Testament, *e. g.* "Depart *from* me, for I am a sinful man." (Luke, 5: 8.)

Equally inconclusive is the case of the Ethiopian eunuch baptized by Philip. We read that they "went down both into [*eis*] the water," and again "they were come up out of [*ek*] the water." The first preposition was employed by the Greeks to denote motion towards an object or place, and hence is rendered into English either by "to" or "into." Thus we read that Christ "went up *to* the feast," that Saul "fell *to* the earth," that Peter "came first *to* the Sepulchre, yet went not in." Indeed in the very chapter which informs us that Philip and the eunuch "went *into* the water," this preposition is six times translated "to" and "unto," and only in this single instance "into." So the corresponding word rendered "out of" has the translation "from" twice as often as "out of" throughout the first five books of the New Testament.

Before it can be enjoined upon all Christians to be immersed because Christ was immersed, it must first be proved absolutely that Christ was immersed, while all that can be absolutely proved from the record is that he was baptized *at* Jordan, and that he "went straightway up *from* the water." There is no absolute proof that he went into the water, no absolute proof that if he did go into the water he was immersed in it. If it be still urged that it seems extremely probable that he was immersed, that it is at least a fair inference from the language taken together with the circumstances, I reply that no man may build a doctrine as to the mode of baptism upon an inference. No barrier may be built around a communion-table upon a probability. I must have something more than a probability, however strong, before I may say to my Christian brother, "I am holier than thou; I am entitled to a place at the Lord's table, but you are not."

It should be remembered moreover that the baptism which Christ received was not Christian baptism, but John's baptism. The two were wholly unlike in their import. John's baptism was "baptism unto repentance." Christ's baptism was the "washing of regeneration." John's baptism differed from Christ's baptism just as his teaching differed from Christ's teaching. John said, "Do justly;" Christ said, "Be born again." The one taught good works, the other regeneration. The one gave the utterance of the law, the other of the gospel. And the baptism of John, like his preaching, belonged to the Old Dispensation; it was the last stage in the long series of legal purifications preparatory to the coming of the Messiah. John himself knew that his baptism differed from that of Christ in that it did not, and could not, represent the inward regeneration of the soul by the Holy Ghost. "I indeed," said he, "baptize you with water, . . . but he that cometh after me shall baptize you with the Holy Ghost." This view is sustained by the ablest commentators. Ohlsausen says, "It is evident that the baptism of John cannot be identical with the sacrament of baptism, which was not ordained till after the resurrection." So Lange, "John's baptism could only purify externally (legally). Christ's baptism is the sign and seal of the inward baptism of the Spirit, which purifies internally." But we have upon this point a better than any human commentary. In Acts, 19: 1—6, we learn, that Paul coming to Ephesus, and finding certain disciples, said to them, "Have ye received the Holy Ghost since ye believed? And they said unto him,

We have not so much as heard whether there be any Holy Ghost. And he said unto them, Unto what then were ye baptized? And they said, Unto John's baptism." Then Paul explained to them the nature of John's baptism, after which he administered to them the ordinance of Christain baptism, showing conclusively that the two were not identical. The baptism which Christ received was John's baptism, and if it could be proved, as it cannot, that the mode of that baptism was immersion, that proof would fall very far short of determining the mode of Christian baptism.

Still farther, if it could be shown, as it cannot, that our Lord received the sacrament of Christian baptism, and if it were demonstrated, as it is not, that he received that baptism by immersion, all this would not show that he intended to prescribe that mode, and enjoin it upon all his followers in all lands and for all time.

There can be no stronger reason why we should imitate the precise mode in which Christ received the ordinance of baptism, than why we should imitate the precise mode in which he observed the Last Supper. He ate that supper in the night, in an upper chamber, himself and apostles reclining on couches around a table, eating unleavened bread. Now, if the exact mode be important in one ordinance, why not in the other? If our Baptist brethren insist that we must be baptized in the same mode in which Christ was baptized, why may we not insist that they should eat the Lord's Supper in the precise mode in which Christ ate it? If you ask them why they do not eat the Sacrament in the night, and in an upper chamber, they will reply, "It is more convenient to celebrate it in the church and in the day time. We do not suppose that Christ meant to insist on those particulars. We feel that we are observing the ordinance in the spirit in which it was given, though not in the precise form." Then we say, "Suppose you prove that Christ was immersed, which you have not done and can not do, we say that it is more convenient to baptize in another mode, and more fitting. We do not suppose that Christ meant to insist on this particular of going into the water. We feel that we are observing the ordinance in the spirit in which it was given, even though it be not in the precise form." If the reason be good for deviation from the precise mode in the one ordinance, why is it not good in the other?

An argument for immersion has been drawn from the passage in John, 3: 23, which states that "John was baptizing in Aenon, because there was much water there." The original, however, reads "many waters there." The name Aenon itself is simply the Greek form of the Chaldee word for fountains. It was a place of springs, or many waters. No traveler in the East halts for a single night, if he can avoid it, without pitching his tent near a spring or stream. The multitudes who flocked to John's teaching made it essential that there should be a supply of water for themselves and beasts. The passage is very far from proving that John baptized by immersion. Far less does it prove that immersion was enjoined upon all Christians.

Allusion is often made to the phrase, "buried with Christ in baptism"—Rom., 6: 4. The whole passage is figurative, and it needs only to be said that if the figure is to be taken literally in one clause, it must be taken literally in all. The previous verse says, "We are baptized into his death." The following verses speak of us as "planted" with Christ, and "crucified with him." If the death is a literal death, if the planting is a literal planting, and the crucifixion a literal crucifixion, then the burial is a literal burial; otherwise not. In point of fact, the passage contains no reference to water-baptism whatever. The reference is to the inner baptism of regeneration, by which we are spiritually identified with Christ in his sufferings and death and resurrection.

Thus these passages, so much relied upon as establishing immersion when examined are not found to establish it. There is not one instance in the New Testament in which immersion can be proved beyond a doubt to have been practised. You may say that it seems extremely probable that immersion was employed in some of these instances. I reply there is not one in which you can absolutely prove that it was employed. Far less can it be shown that Christ prescribed this mode for all his followers.

I have already said that his was to be a universal religion. His spiritual worship was to go over the entire earth, and in connection with it he taught his followers two simple rites; they were to be baptized with water; they were to break the bread and pour the wine in remembrance of him. Nothing was said as to the precise mode in which either of these ordinances was to be kept, but we may be sure that, designing them to be of universal application, he would enjoin for them no mode which was not capable of universal application. Baptism, as Christ well knew, was to be administered not only in the hot country where he dwelt, and where ablutions were frequent and necessary, but in the cold latitudes of perpetual ice,* and in the sick room, where the shadow of death had already come. It is an impeachment of the

* As these words are being placed in type, there comes a commentary upon them in the form of a complaint, uttered by one of the correspondents of the New York *Tribune*, who writes to protest, in the name of humanity, against the terrible exposure incident to immersion as practised in the Adirondack region in winter. "On bitter cold days," says this indignant correspondent, "with the thermometer at zero, the rough rivers, hid in thick ice, are bared with ax and spade, and the converts—often sweet young girls of tender age—are plunged in. As we see them struggling in evident fear and agony, shrinking from their water-soaked garments, which freeze about them, we can but ask if *this* be imitating the blessed Master? Had Christ preached and baptized in this climate, would he, who healed the sick, have risked the life of the body, to purge out the innocent stains of girlhood? It is one of the inexpressible inconsistencies of weak humanity, that followers of the divine Lord should, in his name, commit cruelties that unbelievers would shrink from." If this be baptism in northern New York, with mercury at zero, what must it be on the coast of Greenland at 60° below zero?

common sense of the Savior, to say that he taught a universal religion, joined with it a rite designed to be of universal application, and then prescribed for it a mode which is incapable of universal application.

Nor is there reason to believe that immersion, whether prescribed for future ages or not, was the mode universally practised by the Apostolic church. Take the instance which occurred at its very threshold, narrated in the second chapter of the Acts, the conversion and baptism of three thousand converts in one day. The scene of this baptism is not at the Jordan, but at Jerusalem. It was in the dry season, "when the day of Pentecost was fully come," or about the 20th of May. The city had no natural supply of water. The "brook Kidron" can scarcely be called a running stream in the rainy season, and in the dry season it is an empty bed of pebbles and sand. The dependance of the people was upon cisterns for private use, upon reservoirs and tanks for the public necessity.* The city was in the hands of the Jewish authorities, who had just put Christ to death, and were full of hatred against the Apostles. Is it probable that the Pharisaic authorities, who even forbade Peter and his fellow-Apostles to teach in their streets, would have permitted them to use any of the public tanks for the immersion of three thousand people.†

This is another difficulty in the case almost as great. Many events were crowded into this memorable day. The disciples met in one place in the

* See Robinson, Bib. Res. in Pal., I., p. 334, et seq.

† A similar difficulty presents itself in regard to the baptism of the eunuch by Philip (Acts, 8 : 26-40). There are no streams in the region referred to. Robinson locates the scene of this baptism at *Wady el-Hasy* for three reasons. (1) It is the nearest point to Azotus on the direct road from Jerusalem to Gaza. (2) There is water there, and no other similar water on the road, "which is *desert*," still, as it was in the days of Philip. In this Wady "a *little water* springs up at intervals. *It can hardly be said to flow, but rather soaks along through the gravel.*" There are deep wells and private cisterns in the villages, but no stream in that (desert) portion of Palestine suitable for immersion. "Down *to*" and "up *from*" some such water both Philip and the eunuch went.—Robinson, Bib. Res., II., 48, 515.

morning; they were filled with the Holy Ghost, and spake in many tongues the wonderful works of God. this miracle was noised abroad in the city. The multitude came together, and Peter preached to them, beginning at nine o'clock. Not only did he utter the discourse given in the narrative, but, as we learn from the 40th verse, "with many other words did he testify and exhort." His discourse was gladly received; men of many nationalities were convinced that Christ, "the desire of all nations," had come. They heard eagerly the new way of salvation, and "about three thousand souls believed." They were baptized and added to the church the same day. Now how much of this wonderful day shall we suppose to have remained for the immersion of these new converts? If we say five hours, and suppose the twelve apostles to have shared in administering the ordinance, they must have immersed six hundred an hour, or fifty apiece, being nearly one a minute, hour after hour!

Nor is this the whole of the difficulty. The chapter closes by saying: "The Lord added unto the church daily such as should be saved." The next chapter gives us another sermon of Peter's, the preaching and teaching continuing till the eventide, at which time Peter and John were arrested. Another multitude was added unto the church, the number of the men being about five thousand. When were these thousands immersed, and where was the water procured for the purpose? If it was proved beyond a doubt, as it is not, that Christ was immersed in the Jordan, would that prove beyond a doubt the immersion at Jerusalem, in the dry season, of these thousands? the first converts received into the church after the ordinance of baptism was instituted, the first fulfillment of the command, "Go ye and teach all nations, baptizing them in the name of the Father, and of the Son, and of the Holy Ghost."

These reasons have we for believing that Christ did not prescribe immersion as the only mode in which baptism should be administered.

IV. A single question remains. If, as I have already shown, Christ did not prescribe any particular mode in which baptism should be administered, why do we adopt the mode of sprinkling? I answer, we do not adopt sprinkling to the exclusion of any other mode. We hold any application of water in the name of the Father, and of the Son, and of the Holy Ghost, to be genuine and valid baptism. We believe that since Christ did not enjoin any mode, his followers are at liberty to employ whatever mode they deem best; the same liberty that is had with reference to the Lord's Supper, which ordinance some receive sitting and others kneeling, some in their pews, others at the altar. We say in the spirit of Paul, "One man esteemeth immersion the only mode, another esteemeth every mode alike. He that immerseth, immerseth to the Lord; he that immerseth not to the Lord he immerseth not. Let every man be fully persuaded in his own mind. The kingdom of God consisteth not of meats and drinks," not in external forms and observances, "but in righteousness and peace and joy in the Holy Ghost." The essential thing in baptism, as our text assures us, is "not the putting away of the filth of the flesh, but the answer of a good conscience towards God." If a man conscientiously feels that he ought to be immersed, we immerse him, just as Paul circumcised Timothy, teaching the meanwhile that "in Christ Jesus neither immersion availeth any thing, neither non-immersion, but a new creature," "for baptism is not that which is outward in the flesh, but baptism is that of the heart."

At the same time using the liberty of choice, which Christ has given his followers, we prefer sprinkling for these reasons:

1. It is convenient.

2. It is capable of universal application. It can go wherever the gospel goes, in Lapland or India, in Nova Zembla or Micronesia. It can be administered in the sick-room or on the couch, from which the be-

lieving spirit is just ready to depart and be with Christ. It can be administered on the desert and in the dungeon. Like the gospel itself, it is fitted for every man, every society, every land.

3. There is yet a deeper reason: Sprinkling, more truly than any other mode, represents outwardly the inner baptism of the soul by the blood of Christ. With great pains-taking, through many centuries of preparation, God created in the Jewish mind a symbolism, which should make the sacrifice of Christ intelligible, when that sacrifice should be offered on Calvary. Sacrifice and blood and cleansing were terms that were planted deep in the Jewish mind, by ages of patient teaching, all looking forward to this grand lesson, with which those ages were to culminate, "the blood of Christ cleanseth from all sin." What now was this symbolism? In Exodus, 24: 6-8 we read:—

"And Moses took half of the blood, and put it in basins; and half of the blood he sprinkled on the altar. And he took the book of the covenant, and read in the audience of the people; and they said, All that the Lord hath said will we do, and be obedient. And Moses took the blood, and sprinkled it on the people, and said, Behold the blood of the covenant, which the Lord hath made with you concerning all these words."

Leviticus 16: 14, 15. "And he shall take of the blood of the bullock, and sprinkle it with his finger upon the mercy seat eastward; and before the mercy seat shall he sprinkle of the blood with his finger seven times. Then shall he kill the goat of the sin offering, that is for the people, and bring his blood within the vail, and do with that blood as he did with the blood of the bullock, and sprinkle it upon the mercy seat, and before the mercy seat."

In the book of Hebrews we have an inspired commentary upon these and similar passages of Exodus and Leviticus, showing that this sprinkling with blood was intended to pre-figure the application of the blood of Christ.

Hebrews 9: 13, 14. "For if the blood of bulls and of goats, and the ashes of a heifer sprinkling the unclean, sanctifieth to the purifying of the flesh: How much more shall the blood of Christ, who through the eternal Spirit offered himself without spot to God, purge your conscience from dead works to serve the living God?" Also, 19—22. "For when Moses had spoken every precept to all the people according to the law, he took the blood of calves and of goats, with water, and scarlet wool, and hyssop, and sprinkled both the book and all the people, saying, This is the blood of the testament which God hath enjoined unto you. Moreover, he sprinkled likewise with blood, both the tabernacle and all the vessels of the ministry. And almost all things are by the law purged with blood; and without shedding of blood is no remission."

Heb. 10: 19—22. "Having, therefore, brethren, boldness to enter into the holiest by the blood of Jesus, By a new and living way, which he hath consecrated for us, through the vail, that is to say, his flesh; And having a high priest over the house of God; Let us draw near with a true heart in full assurance of faith, having our hearts sprinkled from an evil conscience, and our bodies washed with pure water."

Hebrews 12: 24. "And (ye are come) to Jesus, the mediator of the new covenant, and to the blood of sprinkling, that speaketh better things than that of Abel." Comp. also I. Pet., 1: 2.

Now put these things together. If the real baptism be the cleansing of the heart from sin by the blood of Christ, and if the whole Bible from Exodus to Hebrews persistently speaks of the application of that blood under the symbolism of sprinkling, and if water-baptism be the outward sign of that inward cleansing by blood, then sprinkling is the mode of applying water which is the truest symbol of the inward baptism. Or more concisely, water-baptism is the outward sign of blood-baptism. The blood of baptism is named by the Scriptures "the blood of sprinkling," and the corresponding name for the water of baptism is "the water of sprinkling." The blood wherewith the heart is cleansed is never named the blood of immersion; there is nothing in the Old Testament symbolism, or the New Testament interpretation of it, even suggestive of immersion. And to show that the Scriptures themselves carried over this symbolism from the application of blood to that of water, turn to Ezek., 36: 25-27. The prophet is there predicting the regeneration of Israel. "A new heart also will I give you, and a new spirit will I put within you; and I will take away the stony heart out of your flesh, and I will give you a heart of flesh. And I will put my Spirit within you, and cause you to walk in my statutes, and ye shall keep my judgments and do them." Now what is the outward symbol of this inward renewal? "Then will I sprinkle clean water upon you, and ye shall be clean: from all your filthiness, and from all your idols, will I cleanse you."

Now, with these prophecies in their hands and with the Jewish practice of cleansing by sprinkling which had been in use for fourteen hundred years most familiarly in mind, Peter, and James, and John saw the multitude on the day of Pentecost turning unto God. Instantly they understood it as the fulfillment of those prophecies which predicted the remarkable outpouring of the Spirit. The Spirit was poured out, a new heart was given unto thousands, a new spirit put within them. In what mode, then, would Peter be likely to apply water as the outward token of this inward heart cleansing. In the manner indicated both by the ancient prophecy, and by the Jewish method of cleansing? He would "sprinkle clean water upon them." No difficult question as to where water could be found for their immersion was to be settled, nor were weary hours to be spent in the administration of the ordinance. As their hearts had been sprinkled from an evil conscience, so were their bodies sprinkled with clean water. As Moses sprinkled all the people standing before the altar, so were these thousands, gathered from every nation under Heaven, sprinkled as they stood together in the congregation, and received at once into the church. They were "not come unto the mount that might be touched, and that burned with fire," but they were "come unto Jesus, the mediator of the new covenant, and to the blood of sprinkling, that speaketh better things than the blood of Abel." So began the fulfillment of Isaiah's prophecy regarding our Redeemer: "He shall sprinkle many nations."

And still the prophecy is being fulfilled. We, too,

my brethren, humbly confessing our sins, have in like manner come unto Jesus, the mediator of the new covenant. Our souls have been sprinkled with "the blood which cleanseth from all sin," our "hearts sprinkled from an evil conscience," and our bodies "sprinkled with clean water," "in the name of the Father, and of the Son, and of the Holy Ghost." We feel that in obedience to Christ we have "repented and been baptized for the remission of our sins," that we have received both the inner and the outer baptism. We utter no reproach against our brethren in that they conscientiously adopt a different mode, but until they can demonstrate absolutely that immersion was performed at least in a single instance, nay until they can show that Christ makes total submergence in water a condition of *his* fellowship, we shall hold that, in shutting us away from the table of our common Lord, they are responsible for the guilt of schism and separation in the body of Christ.

www.ingramcontent.com/pod-product-compliance
Lightning Source LLC
LaVergne TN
LVHW011139110826
845150LV00008B/2416
* 9 7 8 1 4 1 8 1 9 3 8 0 5 *